Reina Russell

THE HYPO HAVEN

Nourishing Meals to Tame
Reactive Hypoglycemia

By

Reina Russell

Reina Russell

TABLE OF CONTENTS

Reina Russell

INTRODUCTION

Understanding Reactive Hypoglycemia

Welcome to *Sugar-Free Symphony: Delicious

Dishes to Keep Blood Sugar in Check*. Before

we embark on this culinary journey, it's crucial to

lay the foundation for understanding reactive

hypoglycemia—a condition that forms the

backdrop of our culinary exploration.

Reactive hypoglycemia is a metabolic condition

characterized by low blood sugar levels that

typically occur a few hours after consuming a

meal, particularly one high in refined

carbohydrates. This phenomenon can lead to a

range of symptoms, including fatigue, irritability,

4

dizziness, and intense sugar cravings. For those navigating the challenges of reactive hypoglycemia, adopting a sugar-free lifestyle becomes not just a choice but a necessity for well-being.

So, let's embark on this flavorful adventure, armed with knowledge and a commitment to crafting meals that harmonize with your body's need for stability. Welcome to a world where the symphony of flavors meets the science of well-being.

CHAPTER 1

Balanced Beginnings

Breakfast Solutions

In this chapter, we will explore a variety of delicious and nutritious breakfast options that are specifically designed to keep your blood sugar levels in check. Starting your day with a balanced meal is crucial for managing your sugar intake and maintaining stable energy levels throughout the day.

We will discuss the importance of choosing sugar-free ingredients and incorporating high-fiber foods into your breakfast routine. You will

discover creative and flavorful recipes that are
not only satisfying but also promote stable blood
sugar levels.

From hearty egg-based dishes to wholesome
oatmeal variations, this chapter will provide you
with a range of options to suit different tastes and
dietary preferences. We will also explore the
benefits of incorporating protein-rich foods and
healthy fats into your breakfast, as they can help
regulate blood sugar levels and keep you feeling
full and satisfied.

Additionally, we will provide tips on meal
prepping breakfast options, so you can save time
and ensure you always have a nutritious meal

ready to start your day. Whether you prefer quick
and easy recipes or enjoy spending time in the
kitchen.

By incorporating these balanced breakfast
solutions into your daily routine, you will not
only enjoy delicious meals but also maintain
stable blood sugar levels, promoting overall
health and well-being.

Energizing Smoothie Bowls
A Symphony of Nutrient-Rich Delight

Welcome to a crescendo of vitality with our
Energizing Smoothie Bowls – a virtuoso
performance in the symphony of balanced

breakfasts for those seeking to keep their blood sugar in check. These delightful bowls are not just a feast for the senses but a nutritional powerhouse crafted to provide sustained energy and stability throughout the day.

Ingredients:

Base:

- 1 cup of low-glycemic fruits (e.g., berries, cherries, or kiwi)

- 1/2 cup of leafy greens (e.g., spinach or kale)

- 1/2 avocado for creaminess

- 1/2 cup of unsweetened almond milk or Greek yogurt

- Ice cubes (optional)

Toppings:

- 1 tablespoon of chia seeds or flaxseeds

- Handful of fresh berries

- Sliced almonds or walnuts for crunch

- Unsweetened coconut flakes

- Drizzle of sugar-free nut butter

Instructions:

1. Blend the Base:

   - In a high-speed blender, combine the low-glycemic fruits, leafy greens, avocado, and almond milk (or yogurt).

   - If desired, add ice cubes for a refreshing chill.

   - Blend until smooth, achieving a thick and creamy consistency.

2. Prepare the Toppings:

   - In a separate bowl, mix chia seeds or flax seeds with a small amount of water and let them sit for a few minutes until they form a gel-like consistency.

   - Arrange the fresh berries, nuts, coconut flakes, and nut butter for topping.

3. Assemble the Bowl:

   - Pour the smoothie base into a bowl, ensuring an even distribution.

   - Add dollops of the chia or flax seed mixture on top.

   - Decorate with the prepared toppings, creating a visually appealing arrangement.

Benefits of Energizing Smoothie Bowls:

Sustained Energy: The combination of low-glycemic fruits, healthy fats from avocado, and protein from nuts provides a gradual release of energy, avoiding blood sugar spikes.

Nutrient-Rich Goodness: Packed with vitamins, minerals, and antioxidants from a variety of fruits and greens, contributing to overall health and well-being.

Balanced Macro-nutrients: A harmonious blend of carbohydrates, fats, and proteins, promoting satiety and keeping you full until your next meal.

Improved Digestion: The fiber from fruits and seeds aids in digestion, supporting a healthy gut and stable blood sugar levels.

Embrace the symphony of flavors and benefits as you indulge in these Energizing Smoothie Bowls—a delicious and nutritious way to kick-start your day with stability and vitality.

Protein-Packed Pancakes

In the symphony of balanced breakfasts, our "Protein-Packed Pancakes" take center stage, offering a delightful harmony of flavors, nutrients, and stability for those managing reactive hypoglycemia. These pancakes are not only a treat for your taste buds but also a nourishing composition designed to keep your blood sugar in check.

Ingredients:

- 1 cup almond flour

- 1/2 cup unsweetened protein powder (plant-based or whey)

- 1 teaspoon baking powder

- 1/4 teaspoon salt

- 2 large eggs

- 1/2 cup unsweetened almond milk (or any non-dairy milk)

- 1 teaspoon vanilla extract

- Optional: Stevia or erythritol for sweetness (to taste)

- Coconut oil or cooking spray for the pan

Instructions:

1. Mix Dry Ingredients:

In a mixing bowl, combine almond flour, protein powder, baking powder, and salt. Stir until well combined.

2. Whisk Wet Ingredients:

In a separate bowl, whisk together eggs, almond milk, and vanilla extract. If you prefer a sweeter taste, add stevia or erythritol to the wet mixture.

3. Combine Mixtures:

Pour the wet ingredients into the dry ingredients, stirring until a smooth batter forms. Allow the batter to rest for a few minutes to thicken.

4. Preheat Pan:

Heat a non-stick skillet or griddle over medium heat and add coconut oil or cooking spray.

5. Cook Pancakes:

Pour 1/4 cup of batter onto the skillet for each pancake. Cook until bubbles form on the surface, then flip and cook the other side until golden brown.

6. Serve Warm:

Stack your protein-packed pancakes and serve warm. Top with fresh berries, a dollop of Greek yogurt, or a sprinkle of chopped nuts for added texture.

Benefits:

1. Stabilized Energy:

The combination of almond flour and protein powder provides a slow and steady release of energy, preventing rapid spikes in blood sugar levels.

2. Satiety and Fullness:

The protein content in these pancakes promotes a feeling of fullness, helping you stay satisfied throughout the morning and reducing the temptation for mid-morning snacks.

3. Nutrient-Rich Goodness:

Almond flour adds a dose of healthy fats and micro-nutrients, contributing to the overall nutritional profile of these pancakes.

4. Deliciously Sugar-Free:

By excluding refined sugars and relying on natural sweetness from ingredients, these pancakes allow you to enjoy a tasty breakfast without compromising your blood sugar stability.

Avocado and Egg Breakfast

Avocado and Egg Breakfast Wraps are a delicious and nutritious option for those looking to keep their blood sugar in check.

Ingredients:

- 2 large eggs

- 1 ripe avocado

- 2 whole wheat tortillas

- Salt and pepper to taste

- Optional toppings: diced tomatoes, chopped

cilantro, hot sauce

Instructions:

1. Heat a non-stick skillet over medium heat.

2. Crack the eggs into a bowl and whisk them

together until well beaten.

3. Slice the avocado in half, remove the pit, and

scoop out the flesh into a small bowl. Mash the

avocado with a fork until smooth.

4. Place the tortillas in the skillet and warm them for about 30 seconds on each side.

5. Remove the tortillas from the skillet and spread half of the mashed avocado onto each tortilla.

6. Pour the beaten eggs into the skillet and cook, stirring occasionally, until they are scrambled and fully cooked.

7. Divide the scrambled eggs evenly between the two tortillas, placing them on top of the mashed avocado.

8. Season with salt and pepper to taste, and add any optional toppings you desire.

9. Roll up the tortillas tightly, tucking in the sides as you go.

10. Serve immediately and enjoy!

Benefits:

- Avocado is a great source of healthy fats, which can help stabilize blood sugar levels and promote satiety.

- Eggs are a good source of protein, which can help regulate blood sugar and keep you feeling full.

- Whole wheat tortillas provide complex carbohydrates, which are digested more slowly and have a lower impact on blood sugar compared to refined grains.

CHAPTER 2

Midday Harmony

Lunchtime Delights.

As the sun climbs higher in the sky, our culinary

symphony continues with the second movement,

we explore lunchtime solutions that not only

satisfy your taste buds but also maintain the

steady rhythm of your blood sugar levels,

ensuring a harmonious afternoon ahead.

Quinoa Salad with Roasted Veggies

Ingredients:

- 1 cup cooked quinoa

- 1 cup mixed vegetables (such as bell peppers, broccoli, carrots)

- 1/2 cup cooked chicken breast, diced (optional for non-vegetarian version)

- 1/4 cup crumbled feta cheese (optional)

- 2 tablespoons chopped fresh herbs (such as parsley, basil, or cilantro)

- 2 tablespoons lemon juice

- 2 tablespoons extra-virgin olive oil

- Salt and pepper to taste

Instructions:

1. In a large bowl, combine the cooked quinoa, mixed vegetables, diced chicken breast (if using), crumbled feta cheese (if using), and chopped fresh herbs.

2. In a small bowl, whisk together the lemon juice, extra-virgin olive oil, salt, and pepper to make the dressing.

3. Pour the dressing over the quinoa mixture and toss until well combined.

4. Taste and adjust the seasoning if needed.

5. Divide the mixture into individual lunch containers or plates.

6. Serve immediately or refrigerate for later use.

Benefits:

- Quinoa is a low-glycemic index grain that provides complex carbohydrates, fiber, and protein, which can help regulate blood sugar levels and keep you feeling full.

- Mixed vegetables add essential vitamins, minerals, and fiber to the dish, promoting overall health and blood sugar control.

- Chicken breast (optional) is a lean source of protein that can help stabilize blood sugar levels and provide satiety.

- Feta cheese (optional) adds a burst of flavor and a small amount of protein to the dish.

- Fresh herbs not only enhance the taste but also provide antioxidants and other beneficial compounds.

Grilled Chicken Lettuce

Grilled Chicken Lettuce Wraps are a delicious and healthy option for those looking to keep their blood sugar in check.

Ingredients:

- 1 pound boneless, skinless chicken breasts

- 2 tablespoons olive oil

- 2 cloves garlic, minced

- 1 teaspoon ground cumin

- 1 teaspoon paprika

- Salt and pepper to taste

- 8 large lettuce leaves (such as romaine or butter lettuce)

- 1 cup diced tomatoes

- 1/2 cup diced cucumbers

- 1/4 cup diced red onions

- 1/4 cup chopped fresh cilantro

- Juice of 1 lime

- Optional toppings: avocado slices, Greek yogurt

(as a substitute for sour cream)

Instructions:

1. Preheat your grill or grill pan over medium-

high heat.

2. In a small bowl, mix together the olive oil,

minced garlic, ground cumin, paprika, salt, and

pepper.

3. Brush the chicken breasts with the prepared

marinade on both sides.

4. Grill the chicken for about 6-8 minutes per side, or until cooked through and no longer pink in the center.

5. Remove the chicken from the grill and let it rest for a few minutes. Then, slice it into thin strips.

6. Assemble the lettuce wraps by placing a few slices of grilled chicken onto each lettuce leaf.

7. Top with diced tomatoes, cucumbers, red onions, and fresh cilantro.

8. Squeeze lime juice over the wraps for added flavor.

9. If desired, add optional toppings such as avocado slices or a dollop of Greek yogurt.

10. Serve immediately and enjoy!

Benefits:

- Low in carbohydrates: Lettuce wraps are a great alternative to traditional wraps or bread, as they are low in carbohydrates. This can help keep blood sugar levels stable.

- High in protein: Grilled chicken is a lean source of protein, which can help promote satiety and support healthy blood sugar levels.

Lentil and Vegetable Soup

Ingredients:

- 1 cup dried lentils

- 1 tablespoon olive oil

- 1 onion, chopped

- 2 cloves garlic, minced

- 2 carrots, diced

- 2 celery stalks, diced

- 1 bell pepper, diced

- 1 zucchini, diced

- 4 cups vegetable broth

- 1 can diced tomatoes

- 1 teaspoon dried thyme

- 1 teaspoon dried oregano

- Salt and pepper to taste

Instructions:

1. Rinse the lentils under cold water and set aside.

2. In a large pot, heat the olive oil over medium heat. Add the onion and garlic, and sauté until fragrant and translucent.

3. Add the carrots, celery, bell pepper, and zucchini to the pot. Cook for about 5 minutes, until the vegetables start to soften.

4. Add the lentils, vegetable broth, diced tomatoes (with their juice), dried thyme, and dried oregano to the pot. Stir well to combine.

5. Bring the soup to a boil, then reduce the heat to low. Cover and simmer for about 30-40 minutes, or until the lentils are tender.

6. Season with salt and pepper to taste.

7. Serve hot and enjoy!

Benefits:

- Lentils are a great source of plant-based protein and fiber, which can help regulate blood sugar levels.

- The vegetables in this soup provide essential vitamins, minerals, and antioxidants, promoting overall health and well-being.
- The low glycemic index of lentils and vegetables makes this soup suitable for individuals looking to manage their blood sugar levels.
- The soup is also low in added sugars, making it a healthy option for those following a sugar-free diet.

CHAPTER 3

Sunset Serenity

Dinner Recipes for Stability

Baked Salmon with Lemon and Dill

Ingredients:

- 4 salmon fillets (about 6 ounces each)

- 2 lemons, sliced

- Fresh dill, chopped

- Salt and pepper, to taste

- Olive oil, for drizzling

Instructions:

1. Preheat your oven to 375°F (190°C) and line a baking sheet with parchment paper.

2. Place the salmon fillets on the prepared baking sheet and season them with salt and pepper.

3. Lay a few slices of lemon on top of each fillet and sprinkle them with fresh dill.

4. Drizzle a little olive oil over the salmon to keep it moist during baking.

5. Bake the salmon in the preheated oven for about 12-15 minutes, or until it flakes easily with a fork.

6. Once cooked, remove the salmon from the oven and let it rest for a few minutes before serving.

7. Serve the baked salmon with lemon and dill alongside your favorite low-carb side dishes or a fresh salad.

Benefits:

- Salmon is an excellent source of high-quality protein, which helps to keep you feeling full and satisfied.

- It is rich in omega-3 fatty acids, which have been shown to have numerous health benefits, including reducing inflammation and improving heart health.

- Lemon adds a refreshing citrus flavor and is a good source of vitamin C, which supports a healthy immune system.

- Dill not only enhances the taste of the dish but also provides antioxidants and may have anti-inflammatory properties.

Zucchini Noodles with Pesto

Ingredients:

- 4 medium zucchini

- 1 cup fresh basil leaves

- 1/4 cup pine nuts

- 2 cloves garlic

- 1/4 cup grated Parmesan cheese (optional)

- 1/4 cup extra virgin olive oil

- Salt and pepper, to taste

- Cherry tomatoes, halved (optional, for garnish)

Instructions:

1. Using a spiralizer or a vegetable peeler, create zucchini noodles by cutting the zucchini into thin, noodle-like strips. Set aside.

2. In a food processor or blender, combine the basil leaves, pine nuts, garlic, and Parmesan cheese (if using). Pulse until the ingredients are finely chopped.

3. Slowly drizzle in the olive oil while the food processor or blender is running until the mixture becomes a smooth pesto sauce. Season with salt and pepper to taste.

4. In a large skillet, heat a little olive oil over medium heat. Add the zucchini noodles and sauté for 2-3 minutes until they are just tender.

5. Remove the skillet from the heat and toss the zucchini noodles with the pesto sauce until well coated.

6. Serve the zucchini noodles with pesto in bowls, garnished with halved cherry tomatoes if desired.

Benefits:

- Zucchini noodles are a great low-carb alternative to traditional pasta, making them suitable for individuals looking to manage their blood sugar levels.

- Zucchini is rich in fiber, which can help regulate blood sugar levels and promote a feeling of fullness.

- Basil is a herb that adds flavor to the dish and contains antioxidants that may help reduce inflammation.

- Pine nuts are a good source of healthy fats and protein, which can help stabilize blood sugar levels and keep you satisfied.

- Olive oil is a heart-healthy fat that provides a source of monounsaturated fats and antioxidants.

- Cherry tomatoes add a burst of color and are low in carbohydrates, making them a suitable addition to a sugar-free dish.

Turkey and Sweet Potato Skillet

Turkey and Sweet Potato Skillet is a delicious and nutritious dish that can help keep blood sugar levels in check.

Ingredients:

- 1 pound ground turkey

- 2 medium sweet potatoes, peeled and diced

- 1 onion, diced

- 2 cloves of garlic, minced

- 1 red bell pepper, diced

- 1 teaspoon ground cumin

- 1 teaspoon paprika

- 1/2 teaspoon dried oregano

- Salt and pepper to taste

- 2 tablespoons olive oil

- Fresh cilantro, chopped (for garnish)

Instructions:

1. Heat olive oil in a large skillet over medium heat.

2. Add the ground turkey and cook until browned, breaking it up into crumbles.

3. Add the diced sweet potatoes, onion, garlic, and red bell pepper to the skillet. Cook for about 5 minutes, until the vegetables start to soften.

4. Sprinkle the cumin, paprika, dried oregano, salt, and pepper over the mixture. Stir well to combine.

5. Cover the skillet and let it simmer for about 10-15 minutes, or until the sweet potatoes are tender.

6. Remove the skillet from heat and garnish with fresh cilantro before serving.

Benefits:

- Turkey is a lean source of protein, which can help stabilize blood sugar levels and promote satiety.

- Sweet potatoes are a complex carbohydrate that are low on the glycemic index, meaning they have a slower impact on blood sugar levels compared to simple carbohydrates.

- The combination of protein from turkey and fiber from sweet potatoes can help slow down the digestion and absorption of carbohydrates, preventing blood sugar spikes.
- This dish is also packed with vitamins, minerals, and antioxidants from the vegetables, providing additional health benefits.

Chapter 4

Creative Sips

Sugar-Free Beverages

Drinking sugar-free beverages can help you

maintain a stable blood sugar level and prevent

spikes and crashes that can affect your mood,

energy, and health. But sugar-free doesn't have to

mean boring or bland. There are many creative

ways to enjoy delicious drinks without adding

any sugar or artificial sweeteners. Here are some

examples of sugar-free beverages that you can

make at home or order at Starbucks:

Sugar-free London Fog

This is a tea latte made with Earl Grey tea, lavender tea, milk, and sugar-free vanilla syrup. It has a floral and aromatic flavor that can soothe your senses and warm you up. To make it at home, brew a cup of Earl Grey tea and a cup of lavender tea, then mix them together. Add some milk of your choice (almond milk is the lowest in sugar) and a splash of sugar-free vanilla syrup. To order it at Starbucks, ask for a hot Earl Grey tea with steamed milk and sugar-free vanilla syrup.

Chia Seed Coconut & Spinach Smoothie

This is a green smoothie that is packed with fiber,
protein, healthy fats, and antioxidants. It can keep
you full and satisfied for hours and provide you
with essential nutrients. To make it at home,
blend together one cup of unsweetened coconut
milk, one cup of baby spinach, one-fourth cup of
chia seeds, one banana, and some ice. You can
also add some cinnamon or vanilla extract for
extra flavor. To order it at Starbucks, ask for a
custom smoothie with coconut milk, spinach, chia
seeds, and banana.

Sugar-free Aam Panna

This is a traditional Indian drink that is made with raw mangoes, mint leaves, cumin, and salt. It has a tangy and refreshing taste that can cool you down and hydrate you. It can also help with digestion and immunity. To make it at home, peel and chop two raw mangoes and boil them in water until soft. Drain the water and mash the pulp. Add some mint leaves, cumin powder, salt, and water to the pulp and blend well. Refrigerate the mixture and serve chilled with some ice. To order it at Starbucks, ask for a passion tea with no sweetener and a splash of lemonade

Refreshing Cucumber Mint Infused Water

Ingredients:

- 1 cucumber, sliced

- 10-12 fresh mint leaves

- 4 cups of water

- Ice cubes (optional)

Instructions:

1. Wash the cucumber thoroughly and slice it into thin rounds.

2. Rinse the mint leaves under cold water to remove any dirt or impurities.

3. In a pitcher or large jar, add the cucumber slices and mint leaves.

4. Pour the water over the cucumber and mint, ensuring that they are fully submerged.

5. If desired, add ice cubes to make the infused water colder.

6. Stir gently to combine the ingredients.

7. Cover the pitcher or jar and refrigerate for at least 2 hours to allow the flavors to infuse.

8. Serve the cucumber mint infused water chilled and enjoy!

Benefits:

- Hydration: Cucumber mint infused water is a refreshing and hydrating beverage that can help quench your thirst.

- Low in Sugar: This sugar-free drink is an excellent alternative to sugary beverages, making

Reina Russell

it suitable for those looking to keep their blood

sugar levels in check.

- Natural Flavor: The combination of cucumber

and mint provides a naturally refreshing and

cooling taste, making it a delightful choice for hot

summer days.

- Antioxidants: Mint leaves contain antioxidants

that can help protect the body against free

radicals and promote overall health.

CONCLUSION

In conclusion, this book is a comprehensive guide that offers a wide range of mouthwatering recipes designed to help individuals maintain stable blood sugar levels while still enjoying delicious meals. Throughout the book, readers have been introduced to the concept of sugar-free cooking and the importance of managing blood sugar levels for overall health and well-being.

The book begins by providing a thorough understanding of blood sugar and its impact on the body. It explains the dangers of excessive sugar consumption and the benefits of adopting a sugar-free lifestyle. It also emphasizes on the importance of making conscious food choices and offers practical tips for reducing sugar intake.

The heart of the book lies in its collection of recipes. Each recipe has been carefully crafted to be both nutritious and delicious, using natural sweeteners and low-glycemic ingredients. From breakfast options like sugar-free pancakes and granola to satisfying main courses such as zucchini noodles with tomato sauce and grilled chicken with roasted vegetables, the book offers a diverse range of dishes to suit every palate.

Moreover, "The Hypo haven" goes beyond just providing recipes. It includes a detailed meal plan that helps readers structure their daily meals and snacks to maintain stable blood sugar levels. The book also offers guidance on portion control and mindful eating, empowering readers to make informed choices about their diet.

This book emphasizes the importance of balance and moderation. While the focus is on sugar-free cooking, the book acknowledges that occasional indulgences are part of a healthy lifestyle. It provides alternatives for satisfying sweet cravings without compromising blood sugar control.

In addition to the recipes and meal plans, it includes valuable information on ingredient substitutions, cooking techniques, and tips for dining out while staying sugar-free. The book is a comprehensive resource that equips readers with

the knowledge and tools they need to make

sustainable changes to their eating habits.

In conclusion, "The Hypo haven" is a valuable

guide for anyone looking to manage their blood

sugar levels while still enjoying flavorful and

satisfying meals. With its wide range of recipes,

meal plans, and practical tips, this book is a must-

have.

Printed in Great Britain
by Amazon